NATURE FILES

ANIMAL CAMOUFLAGE & DEFENSE

Printed and bound in China
10 9 8 7 6 5 4 3 2 1

Library of Congress Cataloging-in-Publication Data applied for.

ISBN: 0-7910-8213-X

Chelsea House Publishers

2080 Cabot Blvd. West, Suite 201
Langhorne, PA 19047-1813

http://www.chelseahouse.com

Produced by

David West 👫 **Children's Books**
7 Princeton Court
55 Felsham Road
London SW15 1AZ

Designer: Julie Joubinaux
Editor: Gail Bushnell
Picture Research: Carlotta Cooper

PHOTO CREDITS :
Abbreviations: t-top, m-middle, b-bottom, r-right, l-left, c-center.

Front cover - all Corbis Images. Pages 3 & 13tl, 10l, 11b, 14b, 15t & b, 22r, 24bl, 25r & bl, 28t, 29b - Corbis Images. 4t, 23mr (Peter Parks), 4b, 18t (Paul Harcourt Davies), 14r (Southampton Oceanography Centre), 16t, 23ml, 28bl (Carlos Villoch), 20t (Chris Parks) - Image Quest 3D. 5t, 7b, 10r, 10–11b, 11t, 12b, 18bl & b, 19r (Pete Oxford), 5b & 10–11t, 9r (Anup Shah), 6t & bl (Doug Wechsler), 6br, 29t (Lynn Stone), 7t (Bristol City Museum), 8m (David Kjaer), 8b (David Welling), 9t (Peter Blackwell), 12tl & tr, 25tl (Jeff Rotman), 13r (Francis Abbott), 13b (Bengt Lundberg), 16b (David Shale), 17t & b (David Hall), 19bl (Staffan Widstrand), 20–21 (Adrian Davies), 21t (Mark Payne Gill), 21b, 27b (Jurgen Freund), 22l (Steve Packman), 23t (Bernard Castelein), 23bl & br, 26t (John Cancalosi), 24t (Dietmar Nill), 24m (Hans Christoph Kappel), 26b (Mary Ann McDonald), 27tl (Tom Vezo), 27m (Brian Lightfoot) - Naturepl.com. 8t (Terry Heathcote), 9m (Paulo de Oliveira), 22b (P.J. De Vries), 9b - Oxford Scientific Films. 19tl, 20b, 27tr - Michael and Patricia Fogden. 28br (Xavier Eichaker) - Still Pictures. 29m - The Culture Archive.

An explanation of difficult words can be found in the glossary on page 31.

NATURE FILES

ANIMAL CAMOUFLAGE & DEFENCE

Kate Petty

CHELSEA HOUSE
PUBLISHERS
A Haights Cross Communications Company

CONTENTS

Only the eyes of the little Sargassum fish are visible as it makes its way through the seaweed of the Sargasso Sea. Several sea creatures are disguised to look like seaweed.

Some well-camouflaged insects are impossible to spot on the plants where they lie in wait for their prey, or stay safely hidden from predators. This is an orchid mantis.

INTRODUCTION

Animals use camouflage to blend into the background and become invisible to their predators or their prey. In the process, some of nature's most cunning disguises are brought into play, by insects that look like plants, lizards that can change color in minutes, large striped mammals that melt into the shadows of the forest, and many more. Other animals may have to defend themselves by standing out from the crowd.

Chameleons are perhaps the best quick-change artists of them all, masters of colorful camouflage. This one is in the process of changing color to blend in with the background.

A lone Indian tiger on the prowl at sunset. Its victim might be as big as a young elephant, but it will neither see nor hear the deadly hunter approaching through the forest.

HIDE AND SEEK

Most animals need to stay hidden in order to survive, either to catch their next meal or to live another day without being eaten. They have evolved to blend in with their particular habitat.

HOW TO BE INVISIBLE

Silvery fish become invisible by rippling and shining like the water they swim in. Even brightly colored insects can disappear completely against petals that are the same bright color as they are. Bold lines can break up the outline of an animal so it vanishes into the distance.

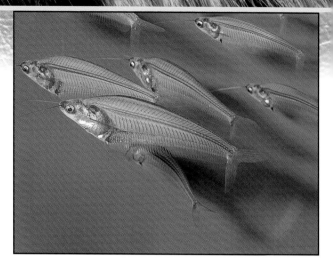

Glass catfish from Southeast Asia are transparent, so their enemies see right through them as they weave among the underwater vegetation.

Even giant pandas can be hard to see.

Amazing FACT

It is hard to believe that the familiar black and white form of the giant panda could ever be hard to spot. In fact, the big patches of black and white make the panda disappear in the snowy mountains in winter. Even in summer, its outline is broken up and difficult to pick out in the bamboo forest.

A goldenrod crab spider. Crab spiders do not make webs, but hide on flowers that are the same color as they are. They pounce on insects as they land.

PEPPERED MOTHS

The camouflage patterns of peppered moths show evolution in action. Once, the pale gray moths were invisible against their tree bark habitat, but as pollution made the bark darker during the 19th century, the paler moths were picked off by birds. Over the years, only the darker moths survived to breed.

HIDDEN AMPHIBIANS

Soft-bodied frogs and toads make tasty mouthfuls for all sorts of birds and other animals. Their survival depends on their blending in well with the rocks and rivers they inhabit. Pattern and color are both important aspects of their camouflage. Amphibians that live mostly on land, such as the Surinam horned frog, are likewise patterned and colored to match their surroundings—in this case, the dead leaves of the forest floor.

A Surinam horned frog digs its body into the forest floor to lie in wait for its next meal. It reacts to movement by leaping up to catch its prey.

7

BABY FACES

Baby animals are particularly at risk from predators. Their camouflage coloring is often what makes them look different from their parents.

UNDERCOVER EGGS

Birds' eggs are harder to find if they have mottled shells. Eggs laid in the open usually resemble the surrounding stones and pebbles. Eggs laid in concealed places, such as underground or very high up, do not need camouflage in the same way.

Kingfishers lay their eggs in burrows, so no camouflage is required. The shells are white, which probably also helps the parents to locate them easily in the dark tunnel.

Parent ringed plovers will distract a predator away from the open nest, knowing that their perfectly camouflaged eggs are even harder to see when left unprotected.

A mother lion has to leave her young cubs unprotected when she goes off to hunt for food, but they are very well camouflaged on the golden plains.

EXTRA SPOTS

Dappled fur keeps many baby animals safely hidden as they lie sleeping. A group of brown and white spotted fawns blend in so well with the leaves and shadows that they are almost impossible to see. Once the young animals are up and running, they still need their protective coloring for some weeks. Even fierce predators are vulnerable when they are young. Lion cubs keep their spotted baby fur for at least three months.

A baby cheetah has a spotted coat and an extra fluffy grayish mane that covers its head, neck, back, and tail, to hide it in the long undergrowth.

Amazing FACT

Looking like a fruit, this "oak apple" is, in fact, a wasp nursery. The mother gall wasp lays her eggs in an oak bud, which then swells to provide food for the larvae when they hatch. Once grown, the adult wasps burrow their way out.

A gall wasp and gall on an oak tree

Hunters and prey both need to blend into the landscape using camouflage. Hunters need to creep up on their prey, while their victims can only survive by remaining hidden.

MATCHING COLORS

In open spaces, both predators and prey tend to be the same colors. The lions and antelope of the savannah are both tawny. Many desert snakes are sand-colored like their victims. In the Arctic, foxes and hares both have white fur.

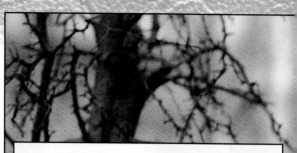

Small herds of gemsbok look for food together in the semidesert of southern Africa. They blend in with the dry earth and stark vegetation.

Amazing FACT

The green vine snake lives in the jungles of southern Asia. With its narrow body, whip-like tail and horizontal pupils, it looks like the creepers and vines it coils around. It strikes out at passing lizards and small birds, which it kills by constriction.

A vine snake

Lionesses slink silently through the yellow grass as they creep up on their prey. They move forward little by little, getting as close to the herd as they can before breaking cover and charging at 40 miles (65 km) per hour.

The tigress's dark stripes match the flickering light and shade of the forest and are protective coloring as she hunts on the jungle floor. The spots of the leopard (inset), basking in a tree, are just like the dappled shadows made by sunlight coming through the leaves.

Zebra stripes do not look like camouflage, but they make it hard for predators with no color vision to single out animals from the herd.

SPOTS AND STRIPES

Spots and stripes give animals what is called "disruptive coloration." Although they look bold, the black markings break up a distinctive body outline, so it is hard to tell if the animal is large or small, or whether there is one animal or several.

ALL CHANGE

How do animals stay camouflaged if their surroundings are always changing? Some animals can change the color of their skins or coats when required.

QUICK-CHANGE ARTISTS

Chameleons make extraordinary transformations in minutes, but a cuttlefish, which is a member of the octopus family, changes color to match the seabed in seconds. Male cuttlefish attract females by changing color several times.

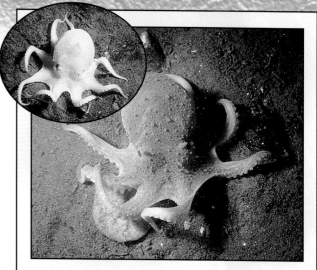

An Atlantic octopus changing color

Amazing FACT

Octopuses and squid change color according to their mood as well as their background. An angry octopus is red, while a frightened one is white. When fighting, they change color constantly between a dark and a pale reddish-brown.

CHAMELEON

The chameleon lives in trees and hunts insects. Effective camouflage keeps it hidden as it lies still and focuses its swiveling eyes on its prey, before capturing it with its long, sticky tongue. Dark pigment (color) stored below the skin can be moved up to each part of the skin surface by impulses from the nerves that serve it.

This is a panther chameleon from Madagascar, a tropical island full of bright colors. Many chameleon species live there.

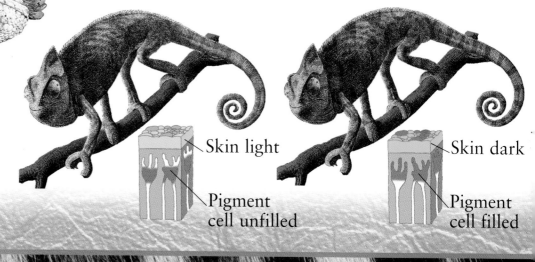

Skin light

Pigment cell unfilled

Skin dark

Pigment cell filled

Flounders change color to match the sea floor exactly, using pigment cells in their skin. Experiments have shown that they can even change to match a chess board!

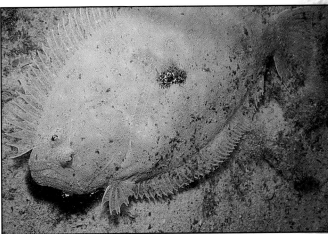

WINTER COATS

Snow changes the scenery dramatically. Arctic animals that are invisible against the dark earth need to change their coats to white. The normally dark-feathered ptarmigan's winter plumage makes it look just like a small snowdrift. Stoats and weasels in places with snowy winters also change color, while those in warmer climates stay brown.

The fur of an Arctic fox changes color with the seasons, always starting with the tail. In the summer, the fox is brown and in autumn, it is white underneath, but still brown on top. The dense winter coat is completely white, keeping the fox warm in temperatures as low as –94 °F (–70 °C).

13

UNDERWATER DISGUISES

Fish are well adapted to the particular depth of the ocean they inhabit, whether it is near the bright surface, in the colder lower parts where light still penetrates, or in the dark, mysterious deep. They all make use of light and color to confuse predators and prey.

LIGHT SHOW

Mackerel, herring, and other fish that swim in schools near the surface are often silver, so their flickering bodies dazzle, like light shining on water. The light organs on dark-colored deep-sea dwellers confuse their prey.

Amazing FACT

Brightly colored butterfly fish live on coral reefs where there are predators such as sharks, octopuses, and fierce moray eels. Stripes break up the outline of this butterfly fish, but it also has a huge false eyespot, located well away from its real eye, to confuse its enemies. It is hard to tell which way it is facing.

This fearsome-looking deep-sea angler fish is only about 6 inches (15 cm) long. The light on the end of its "rod," or lure, attracts smaller creatures. They swim into its mouth and are trapped by its curved teeth.

Flashes of light that reflect from the silvery sides of a school of tuna confuse predators.

A butterfly fish with an eyespot

COLOR ON THE REEF

Coral reefs teem with sea creatures of so many brilliant colors that they all blend in. Bold markings are probably there to help the fish recognize their own species, as well as to camouflage them. In the bright light and deep shadows, the stripes break up their outlines. There are over 200 sorts of butterfly fish alone, all with slightly different stripes and spots.

COUNTERSHADING

Countershading reverses the natural way in which objects are lit from above and are darker underneath. Most fish have countershading so that their upper parts are darker and their bellies are pale, which makes them hard to spot from above or below. Many land animals have countershading, too.

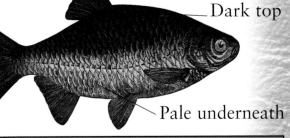
Dark top

Pale underneath

Due to countershading, the shark's sleek outline is almost lost against light from the surface.

Some of the most ingeniously camouflaged underwater creatures manage to look very like the sea plants or stones—or even other sea animals—they live with.

SEAWEED SURPRISE

Fronds of seaweed growing up from the seabed float and drift with the currents. Several sea creatures are colored green-brown like seaweed, and even have waving frond-like extensions to complete the disguise.

The wobbegong shark is almost invisible on the sea bed due to its coloring and the seaweed-like frill around its mouth.

The strangely shaped Sargassum fish (left) lives in the Sargasso Sea, which is full of seaweed. Its body is covered in leaf-like growths and spines.

FLAT FISH CHANGING SHAPE

10 days old—eyes on both sides of head

17 days old—left eye at center of head

Fully grown

13 days old—left eye starts moving upward

35 days old—both eyes on right side of head

Flatfish, such as flounders and plaice, change color to match the seabed. They also change shape as they grow from larvae to fish so they can lie completely flat on the seabed.

One eye actually migrates or moves across the fish's head, so that both eyes of the fully grown fish are on the upper side. This allows the fish to look out for food while lying flat.

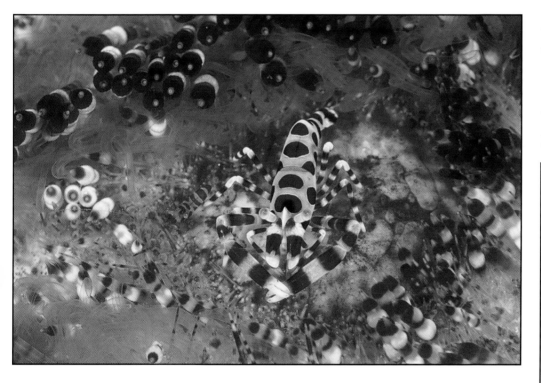

Striped, spiny shrimp fish are related to seahorses. They are invisible among the sea urchins' spines where they live, safe from predators.

Amazing FACT

Possibly the most venomous fish in the world, the stonefish has lethal spines that it raises when it is disturbed. Stonefish are totally invisible on the seabed.

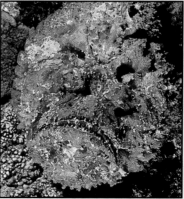

Stonefish are deadly.

LIVING BACKGROUNDS

Sometimes, sea creatures themselves become the background for others to blend in with. The sea urchin is home to tiny shrimp fish that look like its spines. Colorful corals provide a background for fish on the reef. Large dark spots on fish such as the harlequin sweetlips act as disruptive coloration to hide it among the branches of coral.

Animals that have evolved to look exactly like the plants they live in are some of the most fascinating and beautiful in nature.

FLOWERS, LEAVES, AND TWIGS

The insects that imitate twigs and leaves have "cryptic" camouflage that hides their shape. Predators simply cannot see them until they move. Leaf insects look like leaves in every respect, even down to the nibbled edges! The orchid mantis has the precise colors and patterns of the orchid it sits on.

Which is petal and which is insect? The orchid mantis watches and waits, its long forearms ready to grab an unsuspecting victim.

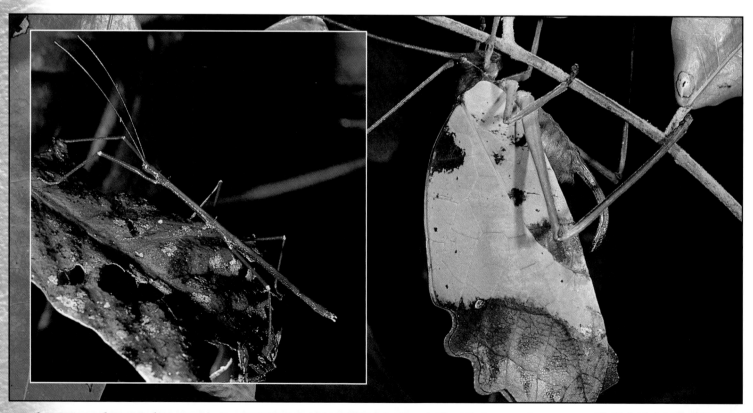

So long as the stick insect (inset) remains still, birds and other predators will think it is a twig. It even changes color according to the light. The leaf-like katydid is a type of cricket.

A sloth covered in algae

Amazing FACT

High up in the rain forest, the three-toed sloth hangs upside-down by its claws and sleeps for two-thirds of the time. Its best protection from eagles and snakes is its camouflage—the green algae that soon covers its fur. The fur grows downward so that rainwater runs off it.

The tail of the leaf-tailed gecko is broad and flat rather than pointed. The shape of its bark-patterned body is disguised by a fringe of scales.

TRUNKS AND BRANCHES

Even large creatures are hard to see if they are the same color as the trees they live in. In the rain forest, sloths look like patches of dappled shade, and vivid green hanging parrots resemble bunches of leaves as they hang upside-down. Insects and small amphibians become invisible on the mottled surface of tree bark.

Stiffening its body to look like a branch completes the disguise of this bird—a tawny frogmouth.

19

These animals are protected by standing out from their surroundings, rather than by blending in with them. Bright colors warn predators that an animal is poisonous.

HAZARD: WARNING SIGNS

Reds, yellows, and blacks are nature's danger signals. Even humans use these colors on warning signs. Spotted red or yellow ladybirds are foul-tasting, and predators soon learn to leave them alone. Yellow and black stripes send out a message to keep away.

A common wasp. The black and yellow stripes of bees, hornets, and wasps warn birds as well as humans that they sting.

The blue-tailed or five-line skink has two sets of warning coloration. If a predator attacks the blue tail, it will drop off, leaving the skink free to run away from danger on its tiny legs.

The fire-bellied toad secretes a poisonous foam. It shows its red and black belly when first threatened, followed by a display of the colored soles of its feet if the attacker persists.

A blue arrow-poison frog

BRIGHT AND BEAUTIFUL

Some of the most strikingly beautiful creatures in nature are brightly colored to scare predators away. Sea slugs on the sea bed have wonderful carnival colors, but their stings are highly toxic. Deadly arrow-poison frogs gleam like shiny little jewels. Fire-bellied toads only show their colorful bellies when under attack.

Amazing FACT

The poison secreted by the vividly colored arrow-poison frog is lethal. Local tribespeople roast the frogs and collect the poison to tip their hunting arrows. The blue arrow-poison frogs from Surinam are both fearless and aggressive. Beware!

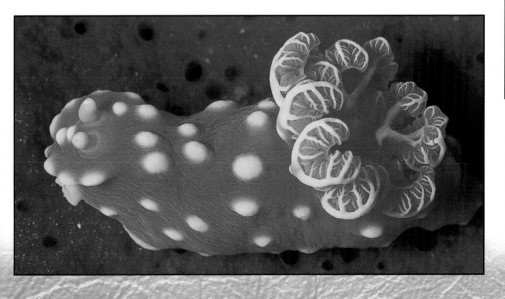

Like land slugs, sea slugs do not have shells. Some sea slugs compensate for their lack of protection with chemical warfare, releasing sulfuric acid into the mouth of an attacker.

21

There are a number of harmless animals that mimic their poisonous doubles exactly. This gives them protection against predators that have learned to avoid brightly colored prey.

Not What They Seem

Hoverflies, wasp-like mimic moths, and wasp beetles are all protected by their yellow and black stripes. Predators avoid insects that mimic foul-tasting ladybirds. Some insects, like ant-mimic spiders, copy their prey, so they can catch them unaware.

The butterfly above is the unpleasant-tasting monarch butterfly. The one below is its harmless mimic, the viceroy butterfly.

Look closely at this "ant" and you will see that it has eight legs. Ant-mimic spiders look and behave like ants, holding up their front legs like feelers, in order to hunt real ants without being noticed.

CONFUSING MIMICS

Animal mimics survive by confusing their predators or their prey. In the case of the coral snake and the king snake, mimicry can confuse humans, too. In the parts of the United States where these snakes are found, locals learn to distinguish the poisonous coral snake (right) from the harmless king snake (left) by remembering: "Red touches black—friend of Jack; red touches yellow—kill a fellow." Look at the stripes and you'll see why.

Amazing FACT

The bee orchid is a flower that mimics an insect! Male bees are attracted to pollinate the bee orchid because it looks—and smells—exactly like a female bee. The pollen sticks to the bee's body when it attempts to mate with the flower.

A bee orchid flower

A predatory fish will not eat the little wrasse that keeps it clean, so the identical-looking blenny (right) is safe.

The coral snake (inset) is very dangerous. The similar-looking king snake is harmless.

SHOCK TACTICS

A brief display of warning colors can deter a predator just long enough for the prey to escape. Many animals use an element of surprise as a defense.

WHAT BIG EYES YOU'VE GOT!

Large eyes usually belong to large birds or mammals, so predators faced with a pair of big "eyes" are likely to leave the prey alone. Eyespots can also focus hunters' attention on less vulnerable parts of the body.

A blue-winged grasshopper moves its front wings forward as it leaps, revealing vivid blue back wings. When it lands, some distance off, it closes them again.

This spicebush swallowtail caterpillar can make itself look scary. It inflates its front end, so the eyespots look like actual big eyes.

The large eyespots on the open wings of a peacock butterfly give the impression of two much larger creatures sitting there. Many butterflies and moths have eyespot patterns on their wings.

SMOKE SCREEN

Cuttlefish, squid, and octopuses can all squirt ink when alarmed, making the water cloudy so they cannot be pursued. Apparently, the ink also distorts the attacker's sense of smell.

Cuttlefish

Ink sac   Gill   Ink squirted out

A giant octopus makes a speedy getaway, leaving a dense trail of blue-black ink.

MORE SURPRISES

It is not only insects that use visual shock tactics. A bright flash of a colored tongue from a skink or a faceful of ink from a squid or an octopus can be enough to scare off many predators. Some prehistoric-looking lizards can suddenly transform themselves into much larger animals by extending their spines or scales.

A blue-tongued skink has a scary tongue.

Amazing FACT

The blue-tongued skink scares predators away by sticking its tongue out at them! The broad, blue tongue emerging from the red mouth is an alarming sight, especially as the skink also puffs itself up and hisses.

The Australian frilled lizard is about 3 feet (1 m) long, with a cloak-like frill round its shoulders. When threatened, it extends the frill outward.

Whether or not they have protective coloring, some animals take positive action to defend themselves. In the case of skunks and tortoises, these defenses are what they are known for.

SPREADING CONFUSION

Lizards and toads often make themselves bigger or taller when threatened. Some animals, like opossums, simply play dead, so predators think they are already dead and leave them alone. Various snakes also play dead.

Amazing FACT

The black and white coat of the common skunk is a warning to other animals to stay away. Skunks store a very unpleasant-smelling liquid in their anal glands, which they can squirt at enemies with terrific accuracy—from as far away as 13 feet (4 m). Animals soon learn to avoid the skunks' territory.

The hognosed snake hisses and spits when first threatened, but then it pretends to die. First, it rolls over. After a few final twitches, it turns rigid and stays that way until the danger has passed.

The bearded dragon from Australia has a spiny pouch under its chin, that expands into a spiky "beard" when the animal is under attack. It also opens its mouth, showing a brightly colored inside.

Threatened skunks lift up their tails.

When threatened by a snake, a toad will inflate itself and rise up on all fours, making it almost impossible for the snake to grip its round body.

A hedgehog rolls into a tight ball to protect itself from enemies. The spines, which are modified hair, stand on end as the muscles below them contract.

TAKING COVER

Spiky or armor-plated animals, like hedgehogs, armadillos, and pangolins, simply curl into a ball to make themselves impenetrable to the enemy. Animals like tortoises and snails can disappear inside their shells.

ARMOR PLATE

A tortoise protects itself by withdrawing into its shell. The outer layer is made of horn sections, called scutes, attached to the flattened bony "carapace," which is fused onto the backbone. The bony bottom half of the shell is called the "plastron."

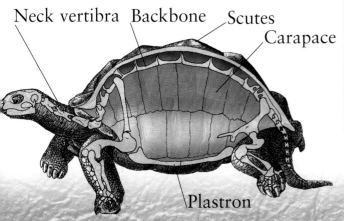

Neck vertibra Backbone Scutes
Carapace
Plastron

Soft-bodied hermit crabs inhabit empty shells. They increase their protection by placing sea anemones with stinging tentacles on top.

Predators know they risk injury or death if they tangle with the spikes and fangs that some animals can wield in self-defense.

STINGS AND VENOM

Stings from insects, jellyfish, and scorpions that are painful to humans can be fatal to smaller creatures, though a venomous bite from some spiders and snakes can kill a human. Animals can use their venom in self-defense, but mostly it is used for paralyzing and killing their prey.

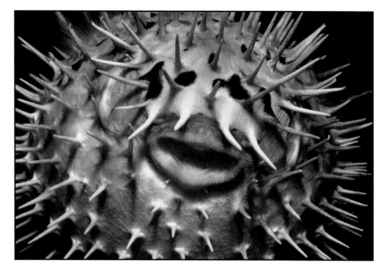

The poisonous puffer fish pumps up its body with water, or sometimes air, when disturbed, transforming itself into a round spiky ball.

POISONOUS SNAKES

A venomous snake injects poison into its victims with its fangs. The venom is stored in glands between its eyes and its mouth. The fangs of a rattlesnake swing forward when it opens its mouth. The venom paralyzes the prey and the snake swallows it whole.

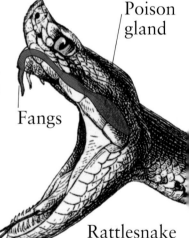

Poison gland

Fangs

Rattlesnake

Most sea creatures on the coral reef steer clear of the stinging tentacles of large sea anemones. Clownfish have a slimy skin that protects them from the stings, so they live in safety from predators among the anemones.

An Egyptian cobra. Cobras have fast-acting venom that paralyzes their victims. A spitting cobra can blind its prey with venom.

SPIKES AND SPINES

The spikes and spines that some mammals are armed with, such as hedgehog prickles, porcupine quills, and rhinoceros horns, are made from modified hair. Baby porcupines are born with all their quills, but they are soft and hair-like to start with. All can inflict some damage, but they are for defense against predators rather than attack.

North American porcupines have up to 30,000 sharp quills on their backs. When threatened, they stamp and rattle their quills, before rushing at the enemy and jabbing it.

The endangered white rhinoceros from Africa has a tough skin and two sharp horns. Unfortunately, poachers still hunt this peaceful creature for the very horn with which it defends itself.

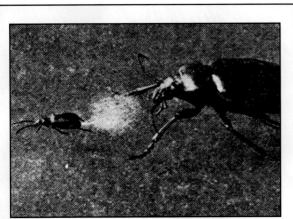

A bombardier beetle

Amazing FACT

The brightly marked bombardier beetle is only 0.6 inch (1.5 cm) long, but if threatened, it aims several shots of boiling hot chemicals straight at its enemy. The mixture explodes from its body in a series of foul-smelling pops as the chemicals, called quinones, make contact with the air.

Hide and seek

• The brown and black diamond patterns of the biggest viper, the gaboon, mean it is completely hidden among the dead leaves on the forest floor, where it curls up, lying in wait for its prey.

Baby cases

• The nymphs of caddisflies live in water and swim around disguised with cases made from grains of sand and bits of plant debris.

Funny disguises

• The South American weevil and the swallowtail butterfly caterpillar are both insects that escape notice by looking just like bird droppings.

Hanging about

• Creatures that live upside down have upside-down countershading! This includes many caterpillars that live upside-down on twigs.

Plant protection

• Thorn treehoppers live in clusters on tropical plants, called lianas. The adults are green and look just like a row of green thorns. The nymphs are brown and lie below them, looking just like the bark.

Mimicry

• The green-blood skink has a green tongue to deter predators, and even has green blood!

Playing dead

• Opossums can "play dead" when under attack. Stress releases substances into the blood, which causes their muscles to contract.

Careful cookery

• Fugu, or puffer fish, is a delicacy in Japan. Specialist cooks have to be carefully trained to remove its deadly poisonous internal organs before cooking.

GLOSSARY

constriction
When a snake squeezes its prey so tightly that it cannot breathe.

countershading
Coloring in which the underside, which is normally in shadow, is paler than the side that is exposed to the light.

cryptic camouflage
Camouflage that disguises the shape of the animal.

disruptive coloration
Patterning, usually black, that breaks up an animal's outline.

endangered
Endangered species are those whose numbers are declining because of over-hunting, loss of habitat, etc.

evolution
A process in which the animals that survive to reproduce are the ones that are the fittest and the strongest.

mimicry
When harmless animals have the same bright coloring as poisonous ones, so that predators will also avoid them.

pollution
Poisoning the air and water with smoke, oil, harmful chemicals, and and other industrial waste.

predator
An animal that hunts and kills other animals for food.

prey
Animals that are hunted by other animals for food.

protective coloring
Coloring that helps an animal blend into its surroundings so that it escapes the notice of predators or prey.

venom
The poisonous fluid injected by some snakes and scorpions when they bite or sting.

31